William Watson

Epigrams of Art, Life, and Nature

William Watson

Epigrams of Art, Life, and Nature

ISBN/EAN: 9783337023782

Printed in Europe, USA, Canada, Australia, Japan

Cover: Foto ©Thomas Meinert / pixelio.de

More available books at **www.hansebooks.com**

EPIGRAMS

OF

ART, LIFE, AND NATURE.

BY

WILLIAM WATSON.

LIVERPOOL:
GILBERT G. WALMSLEY, 50, LORD STREET.

1884

I.

Thou dost but flit, my merle! from tree to tree,
  While on the heights of morn the lark is loud.
Thou hast no wish thy native world to flee,
  Knowing the star is far, and dense the cloud.

II.

In youth the artist voweth lover's vows

To Art, in manhood maketh her his spouse.

Well if her charms yet hold for him such joy

As when he craved some boon and she was coy!

III.

The Poet gathers fruit from every tree,

Yea, grapes from thorns and figs from thistles he.

Pluck'd by his hand, the basest weed that grows

Towers to a lily, reddens to a rose.

IV.

THE PLAY OF "KING LEAR."

Here Love the slain with Love the slayer lies;
    Deep drown'd are both in the same sunless pool.
Up from its depths that mirror thundering skies
    Bubbles the wan mirth of the mirthless Fool.

V.

BYRON THE VOLUPTUARY.

Too avid of earth's bliss, he was of those
    Whom Delight flies because they give her chase.
Only the odour of her wild hair blows
    Back in their faces hungering for her face.

VI.

'Tis human fortune's happiest height, to be

   A spirit melodious, lucid, poised, and whole :

Second in order of felicity

   I hold it, to have walk'd with such a soul.

VII.

I close your Marlowe's page, my Shakspere's ope.

How welcome—after gong and cymbal's din—

The continuity, the long slow slope

And vast curves of the gradual violin!

VIII.

SHELLEY AND HARRIET WESTBROOK.

A great star stoop'd from heaven and loved a flower
Grown in earth's garden—loved it for an hour:
Let eyes which trace his orbit in the spheres
Refuse not, to a ruin'd rosebud, tears.

IX.

DÜRER'S 'MELENCOLIA.'

What holds her fix'd far eyes nor lets them range?
Not the strange sea, strange earth, or heaven more strange;
But her own phantom dwarfing these great three,
More strange than all, more old than heaven, earth, sea.

X.

To Art we go as to a well, athirst,
    And drinking see our shadow, and the sky's,
But wholly 'neath the water must be mers'd
    To clasp the naiad Truth where low she lies.

XI.

The beasts in field are glad, and have not wit
    To know why leap'd their hearts when spring-time shone.
Man looks at his own bliss, considers it,
    Weighs it with curious fingers; and 'tis gone.

XII.

THINKERS, PAST AND PRESENT.

God, by the earlier sceptic, was exiled;
The later is more lenient grown and mild:
He sanctions God, provided you agree
To any other name for deity.

XIII.

TO A POET.

Time, the extortioner, from richest beauty
Takes heavy toll and wrings rapacious duty.
Austere of feature if thou carve thy rhyme,
Perchance 'twill pay the lesser tax to Time.

XIV.

THE YEAR'S MINSTRELSY.

Spring, the low prelude of a lordlier song :

   Summer, a music without hint of death :

Autumn, a cadence lingeringly long :

   Winter, a pause;—the Minstrel-Year takes breath.

XV.

INSCRIPTION ON A ROCK HAVING THE LIKENESS OF IMMENSE HUMAN FEATURES.

The seafowls build in wrinkles of my face.
    Ages ere man was, man was mock'd of me.
Kings fall, gods die, worlds crash;—at my throne's base
    In showers of bright white thunder breaks the sea.

XVI.

KEATS.

He dwelt with the bright gods of elder time,

    On earth and in their cloudy haunts above.

He loved them : and, in recompense sublime,

    The gods, alas ! gave him their fatal love.

XVII.

THE RUINED ABBEY.

Flower-fondled, clasp'd in ivy's close caress,
   It seems allied with Nature, yet apart :—
Of wood's and wave's insensate loveliness
   The glad, sad, tranquil, passionate, human heart.

XVIII.

ANTONY AT ACTIUM.

He holds a dubious balance :—yet *that* scale,

Whose freight the world is, surely shall prevail?

No; Cleopatra droppeth into *this*

One counterpoising orient sultry kiss.

XIX.

BACH, IN THE FUGUES AND PRELUDES.

Contentedly with strictest strands confined,

Sports in the sun that oceanic mind:

To leap their bourn these waves did never long,

Or roll against the stars their rockbound song.

XX.

Nettle and dockleaf ancient neighbours be :

And herb-of-healing jostles bane-berry.

Grows by the bank which Marah's waters lave

The tree that maketh sweet the bitter wave.

XXI.

My friend the apothecary o'er the way

Doth in his window Byron's bust display.

Once, at Childe Harold's voice, did Europe bow:

He wears a patent lung-protector now.

XXII.

FROM THE FRENCH.

Says Marmontel, The secret's mine

Of Racine's art-of-verse divine.

To do thee justice, Marmontel,

Never was secret kept so well.

XXIII.

FROM THE SPANISH.

The Stage is all men's mirror clear.
   They who condemn it, judgment pass
Upon themselves. Who fly it, fear
   To meet their image in the glass.

XXIV.

Momentous to himself as I to me
    Hath each man been that ever woman bore;
Once, in a lightning-flash of sympathy,
    I *felt* this truth, an instant, and no more.

XXV.

What would we here, what would we here at all,—

    Vex'd with the hungering eye and thirsting ear,—

Whirl'd with the whirling of the sleepless ball?

    Behold we know not ev'n what would we here.

XXVI.

Daily by his own hands are writ out fair
    In a great book the great thoughts of the King.
We can but mark the purport here and there
    For very wonder at the handwriting.

XXVII.

If Nature be a phantasm as thou say'st,
  A splendid fiction and prodigious dream,
To reach the real and true I'll make no haste,
  More than content with worlds that only seem.

XXVIII.

BACK FROM ABROAD.

I wearied of that southern sky and main,
  Ocean and heaven one mutual bland blue smile.
Welcome the vapour-tarnish'd crown again
  And wind-torn girdle of our northern isle!

XXIX.

TO ROSSETTI DEAD.

Rich spirit escap'd these mortal hindrances
    And dense impediments of crumbling clay,
To join thy kin thou journeyest : thou from these
    Time-sunder'd wast ; Keats, Dante, Tintoret they.

XXX.

The gods man makes he breaks; proclaims them
  each
  Immortal, and himself outlives them all:
But whom he set not up he cannot reach
  To shake His cloud-dark sun-bright pedestal.

XXXI.

In mid whirl of the dance of Time ye start,
    Start at the cold touch of Eternity,
And cast your cloaks about you, and depart.
    The minstrels pause not in their minstrelsy.

XXXII.

TO EDWARD DOWDEN,

On learning that he was about to be engaged upon the Life of Shelley.

Thy task will yield thee much sad happiness
   With the sea-amorous Ariel, sea-betray'd.
Thyself I gratulate; and him not less,
   The swift wild Sprite, who such a friend hath made!

XXXIII.

MICHELANGELO'S " MOSES."

The captain's might, and mystery of the seer—
Remoteness of Jehovah's colloquist,
Nearness of man's heaven-advocate—are here:
Alone Mount Nebo's harsh foreshadow is miss'd.

XXXIV

ROCHEFOUCAULD CONSISTENT.

Sage Duke, thy creed who runs may read—
Men feign in every word and deed.
Therewith thy practice well agreed,
For sure am I thou feign'dst thy creed.

XXXV.

THE COURSE OF MUSIC.—TO CERTAIN CONTEMPORARY MUSICIANS.

Through Formalism her feet progress—
Reach Form,—yet still would onward press.
There bid her tarry! 'Tis, I guess,
But few steps more to Formlessness.

XXXVI.

Like leaves on the swoln stream of the swift days
 Do all men somewhither move rushingly;
While Man stands at the brink, with eyes that gaze
 Back to the source and forward to the sea.

XXXVII.

To keep in sight Perfection, and adore
   The vision, is the artist's best delight ;
His bitterest pang, that he can ne'er do more
   Than keep her long'd-for loveliness in sight.

XXXVIII.

TWO POETS.

A peacock's-tail-like splendour hath this Muse,
With eyes that see not throng'd, and gorgeous hues.
The swan's white grace that other wears instead,
Stately with stem-like throat and flower-like head.

XXXIX.

"*ON SUCH A NIGHT.*"

On such a night as this, pale Hero found,

By the blown waters, the world's sweetness drown'd.

And all was woe beneath the moonbeam, save

The innumerable laugh of leagues of wave.

XL.

Thou canst not loose the tangles: let them be.

Accept the shadow with the verity.

Aye at one birth, Truth and the Dream are born.

Lo! near the Ivory Gate, the Gate of Horn.

XLI.

The children romp within the graveyard's pale;

The lark sings o'er a madhouse, or a gaol;—

Such nice antitheses of perfect poise

Chance in her curious rhetoric employs.

XLII.

WRITTEN IN A VOLUME OF CHRISTINA G. ROSSETTI'S POEMS.

Songstress, in all times ended and begun,
   Thy billowy-bosom'd fellows are not three.
Of those sweet peers, the grass is green o'er one ;
   And blue above the other is the sea.

XLIII.

THE ALPS.

Adieu, white brows of Europe! sovereign brows,
   That wear the sunset for a golden tiar.
With me in memory shall your phantoms house
   For ever, whiter than yourselves, and higher.

XLIV.

Our lithe thoughts gambol close to God's abyss,

Children whose home is by the precipice.

Fear not thy little ones shall o'er it fall:

Solid, though viewless, is the girdling wall.

XLV.

Lives there whom Pain hath evermore pass'd by

And Sorrow shunn'd with an averted eye?

Him do thou pity, him above the rest,

Him of all hapless mortals most unbless'd.

XLVI.

SHELLEY'S DEATH.

'Twas some enamour'd Nereid craved a storm
   Of Eolus, her minstrel to immerse
In blue cold waves and white caresses warm:
   So the sea whelm'd him, whelming not his verse.

XLVII.

THE CATHEDRAL SPIRE.

It soars like hearts of hapless men who dare
    To sue for gifts the gods refuse to allot ;
Who climb for ever toward they know not where,
    Baffled for ever by they know not what.

XLVIII.

'Tis meet the Poet sometimes walk, unchid,
In vagueness of the word-spun veil half-hid.
'Tis meet the mountain sometimes be allowed
To cloak its heaven-conversant peaks with cloud.

XLIX.

Say what thou wilt, the young are happy never.

Give me bless'd Age, beyond the fire and fever,—

Past the delight that shatters, hope that stings,

And eager flutt'ring of life's ignorant wings.

L.

AN EPITAPH.

His friends he loved. His fellest earthly foes—
  Cats—I believe he did but feign to hate.
My hand will miss the insinuated nose,
  Mine eyes the tail that wagg'd contempt at Fate.

LI.

A MARGINAL NOTE ON "THE TEMPEST."

The Truth is shackles and an iron door.
   In dreams alone we drink of liberty.
For fetters whilst unfelt are bonds no more,
   And free they are who think that they are free.

LII.

Who never knew a sorrow grow his friend

And half regretted from his threshold wend ?

Who never long'd his tear-scorcht eyes to lave

Rather with any than with Lethe's wave ?

LIII.

"How weak are words—to carry thoughts like mine!"
Saith each dull dangler round the much-bored Nine.
Yet words sufficed for Shakspere's suit when he
Woo'd Time, and won instead Eternity.

LIV.

AN ALLEGED CHARACTERISTIC OF GOETHE.

'Tis writ, O Dogs, that Goethe hated you.
I doubt:—for was not he a poet true?
True poets but transcendent lovers be,
And one great love-confession poesy.

LV.

THE TOWN, BY GASLIGHT.

Here age loathes age, and youth doth youth decoy

With pleasure's joyless travesty of joy;

And Sin and Death with link'd arms walk the street;

And night's mad heart doth beat, and beat, and beat.

LVI.

BYRON AND WORDSWORTH.

For Byron, song was an insatiate flame
    To fling his heart in when the world stood by.
To Wordsworth like his mountain brooks it came,
    An earthborn coolness colour'd with the sky.

LVII.

THE METROPOLITAN UNDERGROUND RAILWAY.

Here were a goodly place wherein to die;—
Grown latterly to sudden change averse,
All violent contrasts fain avoid would I
On passing from this world into a worse.

LVIII.

Onward the chariot of the Untarrying moves;

Nor day divulges him nor night conceals;

Thou hear'st the echo of unreturning hooves

And thunder of irrevocable wheels.

LIX.

A deft musician does the breeze become
Whenever an Æolian harp it finds:
Hornpipe and hurdygurdy both are dumb
Unto the most musicianly of winds.

LX.

ON SEEING THE TOMB OF INFANT BROTHERS TWIN-BORN.

Mates of the cradle, fellows of the grave,
   A handbreadth parts them in the mould below ;
Whom, had they lived, perhaps the estranging wave,
   Or hate—or love—had sunder'd wide enow.

LXI.

A MAIDEN'S EPITAPH.

She dwelt among us till the flowers, 'tis said,
   Grew jealous of her: with precipitate feet,
As loth to wrong them unawares, she fled.
   Earth is less fragrant now, and heaven more sweet.

LXII.

I follow Beauty; of her train am I:
   Beauty whose voice is earth and sea and air;
Who serveth, and her hands for all things ply;
   Who reigneth, and her throne is everywhere.

LXIII.

Full high we soar, and dive exceeding deep,
    And tease the gods to fling the unwilling meed ;
And best of guerdons is the grassy sleep
    And dusty end of all our dream and deed.

LXIV.

ON READING HOW THE WIDOW OF WAGNER CUT OFF HER HAIR, AND PLACED IT IN HER HUSBAND'S COFFIN WITH HIS CORPSE.

Her head's bright harvest, shorn, she laid i' the mould,
Flooding death's emptiness with billowy gold.
He sleeps; and in his earthy dreams, can see
Her lustrous love illume eternity.

LXV.

A SOMETIME CONTEMPORARY.

Ah vain, thrice vain in the end, thy rage and hate.

Vain and thrice vain, as all shall see who wait.

For hawk at last shall be outsoar'd by dove,

And throats of thunder quell'd by lips of love.

LXVI.

DARWINISM UPSIDE-DOWN.

The public voice, though faltering, still demurs
To own that men have apes for ancestors.
The inverse marvel fronts me daily, when
I talk with apes whose ancestors were men.

LXVII.

MERLIN.

He—who made Nature jealous with his Art—
He slumbers folded in the oak-tree's heart.
And in his own heart, like a flower night-furl'd,
Slumbers the folded secret of the world.

LXVIII.

Immured in sense, with fivefold bonds confined,
  Rest we content if whispers from the stars
In waftings of the incalculable wind
  Come blown at midnight through our prison-bars.

LXIX.

Once more a perfect morn! With feet that trod
 Earth's green, and sun-kiss'd hair that swept heaven's blue—
Affable, smiling, aweless—I met God,
 Delighted with his work as when 'twas new.

LXX.

BYRON'S "DON JUAN."

One singer loud among our latter quire
   Likens to ocean this expanse of song.
Hoist sail, who would the waves' salt breath inspire!
   But fear a lurch, whose stomachs are not strong.

LXXI.

A HINT TO THE SHADE OF LAMB. *

What! our Inspired Dyspeptic must select
   Thee too, my heart's own Elia, to revile?
Avenge thee, gentle ghost! Rise, and project
   A club of authors all damn'd by Carlyle.

* See his essay embodying the proposal for a club of damned authors.

LXXII.

I know the tenebrous moods that interpose
   Thick solid horror 'twixt our eyes and Day!
Who scape them? Sages? Saints? Perhaps: and
     those
   Rapt hogs, in heaven of hog-swill, o'er the way.

LXXIII.

For metaphors of man we search the skies,
    And find our allegory in all the air.
We gaze on Nature with Narcissus-eyes,
    Enamour'd of our shadow everywhere.

LXXIV.

ART.

The thousand painful steps at last are trod,
    At last the temple's difficult door we win ;
But perfect on his pedestal, the god
    Freezes us hopeless when we enter in.

LXXV.

ON LONGFELLOW'S DEATH.

No puissant singer he, whose silence grieves
    To-day the great West's tender heart and strong;
No singer vast of voice: yet one who leaves
    His native air the sweeter for his song.

LXXVI.

Thou deemest that the soul through death ascends
 To lordlier halls than sumptuous Life doth rule.
They needs were bright and wide, to make amends
 For such a strait and lampless vestibule.

LXXVII.

I roam'd through streets with human ruins strewn
  Where mirthless laughter hid Sin's writhing heart.
The lamps shone round me; o'er me shone the moon :
  And earth and heaven seem'd very wide apart.

LXXVIII.

SHAKSPERE'S POURTRAYAL OF CÆSAR.

With critic eye earth's lordliest soul he scann'd,
And drew the demigod with captious hand.
Perverse! to paint the sunspots every one,
And quite leave out the interlustrous sun.

LXXIX.

TO MR. GLADSTONE (1882).

Sculptor of nobler stuff than marble thou,

Shaping the morrow from the plastic Now.

Fain wouldst thou carve it fair;—alas! what use?

A churl's rais'd foot can mar a Pheidian Zeus.

LXXX.

Love, like a bird, hath perch'd upon a spray
    For thee and me to hearken what he sings.
Contented, he forgets to fly away;
    But hush! . . . remind not Eros of his wings.

LXXXI.

Toiling and yearning, 'tis man's doom to see
   No perfect creature fashion'd of his hands.
Insulted by a flower's immaculacy,
   And mock'd at by the flawless stars he stands.

LXXXII.

TO WALT WHITMAN.

Some find thee foul and rank and fetid, Walt,
Who cannot tell Arabia from a sty.
Thou followest Truth, nor fearest, nor dost halt;
 Truth: and the sole uncleanness is a lie.

LXXXIII.

TO GOETHE.

With earth well pleas'd, thou liv'dst to sing and know;
  Yet somewhat as the stars in thine own song,
That haste not, neither rest, didst o'er it glow:
  A light that, setting, for more light didst long.

LXXXIV.

The statue—Buonarroti said—doth wait,

Thrall'd in the block, for me to emancipate.

The poem—saith the poet—wanders free

Till I betray it to captivity.

LXXXV.

Not yet the ghosts of the old gods are laid.

By the wing'd archer still, youth's wounds are made.

And still in the blue deeps of virgins' eyes

Dances the wave whence Venus did arise.

LXXXVI.

BROWNING.

A lion!—And with such can no beast cope.

The shaggiest lion couch'd on Parnasse' slope.

Entoil'd at times with meshes hard to undo:

Which God inspire the mouse to nibble through!

LXXXVII.

TO A SEABIRD.

Fain would I have thee barter fates with me—
Lone loiterer where the shells like jewels be,
Hung on the fringe and fray'd hem of the sea.
But no!—'twere cruel, white-wing'd Bliss! to thee.

LXXXVIII

"*MANY THINGS ARE GROWING PLAIN AND CLEAR TO ME.*"

(Schiller's Last Words.)

What saw he when this mist of flesh 'gan lift?
Truth like a dawn flame tow'rd him through the rift,
And old ghosts hide them from the wild new gleam.
He wonder'd; and shook off this clinging dream.

LXXXIX.

TANTALUS.

He woo's for ever with foil'd lips of drouth

The wave that wearies not to mock his mouth.

'Tis Lethe's. They alone that tide have quaff'd

Who never thirsted for the oblivious draught.

XC.

Brook, from whose bridge the wandering idler peers
  To watch thy small fish dart or cool floor shine,
I would that bridge whose arches all are years
  Spann'd not a less transparent wave than thine!

XCI.

One music maketh its occult abode
   In all things scatter'd from great Beauty's hand ;
And evermore the deepest words of God
   Are yet the easiest to understand.

XCII.

Enough of mournful melodies, my lute!

Be henceforth joyous, or be henceforth mute.

Song's breath is wasted when it does but fan

The smouldering infelicity of man.

XCIII.

For thee, the gods yet haunt Olympus hill:

Thou seest beside each muse-frequented rill

The twice nine feet of song a-straying still:

For there is nought he may not see, who will.

XCIV.

TO A FOOLISH WISE MAN.

The world's an orange—thou hast suck'd its juice ;
  But wherefore all this pomp and pride and puffing ?
Somehow a goose is none the less a goose
  Though moon and stars be minc'd to yield it stuffing.

XCV.

"SUBJECTIVITY" IN ART.

If, in the Work, must needs stand manifest
  The Person, be his features, therein shown,
Like a man's thought in a god's words express'd—
  His own and somehow greater than his own.

XCVI.

Think not thy wisdom can illume away

The ancient tanglement of night and day.

Enough, to acknowledge both, and both revere:

They see not clearliest who see all things clear.

XCVII.

I pluck'd this flower, O brighter flower, for thee,

There where the river dies into the sea.

To kiss it the wild west wind hath made free :

Kiss it thyself and give it back to me.

XCVIII.

Marr'd is our music by the singer's tears
    And vex'd with tremblings of the harper's hand.
The perfect notes of the symphonious spheres
    Who but the listening stars may understand?

XCIX.

To be as this old elm full loth were I,
   That shakes in the autumn storm its palsied head.
Hewn by the weird last woodman let me lie
   Ere the path rustle with my foliage shed.

C.

His rhymes the poet flings at all men's feet,
   And whoso will may trample on his rhymes.
Should Time let die a song that's true and sweet
   The singer's loss were more than match'd by Time's.

A NOTE ON EPIGRAM.

AS most commonly understood, the Epigram is primarily an instrument of social satire or personal invective—a handy weapon, having the keenness of the stiletto, and its glitter. In our language are some ingenious definitions of its nature and function—themselves examples of what they set out to define—based on the popular tradition of Epigram. Disappointed must any reader have been who looked to find that tradition illustrated throughout the foregoing pages. Poems conformable thereto are here to be found; but they are exceptional, not regular, in the scheme of this volume.

Concerning the nobler sort of Epigram a few words may not be misplaced here; but I make no pretence of tracing its development, or otherwise treating it historically. In that connection it may be sufficient to allude to the fact that the character of the Greek Epigram was early determined by its being originally an INSCRIPTION, then a short poem in Elegiacs, with the qualities of simple beauty and conciseness appropriate to lapidary or monumental uses. All manner of subjects were deemed eligible for treatment in this form, and the Epigram sometimes became a condensed (perhaps a strangulated) lyric. It was in Latin, and with Martial, that its close was first forced into sharp relief. In his hands it was often anything but " a box where sweets compacted lie," but it began to resemble some boxes in its way of shutting with a snap or click. In French literature the Greek example had of course no practical influence, and the Epigram became what Boileau describes :—

" L'épigramme plus libre en son tour, plus borné,
N'est souvent qu'un bon mot de deux rimes orné."

Many lines, and groups of lines, which we are in the habit of quoting from a body of continuous verse, are essentially Epigrams. Sometimes a couplet thus detached and exhibited is made all the more impressive by isolation. Taken together with its context, we see what has led up to it, and *what grows out of it*. Set it apart, and it seems a thing *self-generated, self-sustinent, individually* whole. When Landor says :—

> "*Fears, like the needle verging* to the Pole,
> Tremble and tremble into certainty,"

or when Shakspere says :—

> " They that stand high have many blasts to shake them,
> And when they fall they dash themselves to pieces,"

we feel that in each case a thought has been presented, *metaphorically*, in utmost completeness; not that it is incapable of amplification, only we have an instinct which tells us that any addition of metaphorical detail would be an incumbrance. *These* things are perfect Epigrams. Shelley's image of Life as a splendid discoloration of eternity's pure whiteness, is an Epigram—a magnificent one,—

> " Life, like a dome of many-coloured glass,
> Stains the white radiance of eternity."

But when he adds :—

> " Until death tramples it to fragments,"

he injures by a superfluity what is already complete. The additional circumstance does not support the image (for the image supports itself), but overweights it, disturbing its sublime oneness of impression. The same might also be said of another forcibly compact line of Adonais:—

"Nought we know dies; shall that alone which knows?"

Shelley does not leave it here, but liberates and pursues afresh the already captured quarry, thus:—

"Nought we know dies; shall that alone which knows
Be as a sword consumed before the sheath
With quenchless lightning?"

A fine Epigram is thus made and marred; but of course one has no right to blame Shelley in this instance, for, on the principle laid down in Pope's familiar couplet:—

"In every work regard the writer's end,
Since none can compass more than they intend,"

he is abundantly justified. And indeed no poet that ever sung could be more innocent of epigrammatic intentions than Shelley usually was; for the lyrical temper, of which he was the incarnation, has little in common with the bent towards Epigram; and thus we are not unprepared to find that the least lyrical of modern English poets of the front rank, Walter Savage Landor, was our greatest modern Epigrammatist.

Among Arthur's heroes, it was the mighty Lancelot who—

"*Best clove a king, or caught a butterfly.*"

In a later day it was Landor, the sculptor of Gebir, and Count Julian, who was ablest to mould a Colossus or incise a gem. His best quatrain is also his best known. No other poem in our language contains such "infinite riches" in such "a little room"; yet, packed as are these treasures, they are not crushed.—

"*I strove with none, for none was worth my strife.
Nature I loved, and next to nature, art.
I warm'd both hands before the fire of life:
It sinks; and I am ready to depart.*"

This poem is a condensed autobiography of Landor's outward and inward careers. His intellectual aloofness in the nineteenth century; his disdain of rivalry with contemporaries; his arrogant yet somehow inoffensive self-assertion, the gracious despotism of the man; his passion for art, that true passion for art which is strongest in minds whose passion for nature is yet more strong; his keen zest of existence, long undiminished, but giving place eventually to the tedium vitæ which clouded his final years; lastly, his entire willingness to take leave of this old comrade Life, whose society is not so vivacious as it once was, and whom he half loves, half scorns; all this is here. And together with all this there is perfection of simple verse-craft, unshadowed lucidity of phrase, and completeness of utterance.

Outside Landor, English literature has had hitherto no quatrains comparable for weight and loftiness to his, with, perhaps, the sole exception of the following remarkable "*Epigram on the death of Edward Forbes*," by Sydney Dobell, a poet from whom one could hardly have expected anything so perfect within so strict limits,—a mystic and trancendentalist, accustomed to wed his intensely spiritualised thought to a literary style as efflorescent as that of the Elizabethans, glowing with a richness of decoration not less prodigal than theirs:—

> "*Nature, a jealous mistress, laid him low.*
> *He woo'd and won her; and, by love made bold,*
> *She showed him more than mortal man should know,*
> *Then slew him lest her secret should be told.*"

Scattered here and there, amid the interesting if often unshapely verse of Emerson, we come upon a quatrain or couplet of almost the best gnomic or sententious-oracular sort. Here is a specially beautiful example:—

> "*Thou canst not wave thy staff in air,*
> *Or dip thy paddle in the lake,*
> *But it carves the bow of beauty there,*
> *And the ripples in rhyme the oar forsake.*"

To add anything respecting my own theory or practice of Epigram were superfluous, since that has already spoken in its own cause, successfully or otherwise, throughout a hundred pages. It seemed allowable, however, to cite a few examples—the best to be had—from other writers, in order to make definite my own position with relation to what has been done before in the same field. In English, such precedents are few; but in German there is the Sixth Book of the West-Östlicher Divan, besides many admirable quatrains scattered up and down Goethe's previous writings, and the writings of other German poets; and Oriental literature has its Omar Khay-yam. As for myself, if here and there I have succeeded in arresting some casual wing of thought as it flew, some transient wave of emotion as it subsided, giving to the thought a not futile fixity, a not idle permanence to the emotion, my accomplishment is on the level of my hope.

W. W.

LIVERPOOL,
　November, 1883.

www.ingramcontent.com/pod-product-compliance
Lightning Source LLC
Chambersburg PA
CBHW022146160426
43197CB00009B/1448